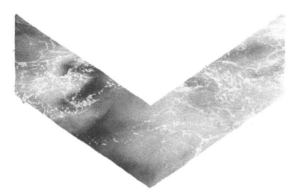

kingdom tide

AWAKENING SERIES · VOLUME THREE

kingdom tide

UNLEASHING THE
RIPPLE EFFECT OF AWAKENING

Matt LeRoy

Printed in the United States of America

Cover and page design by Strange Last Name
Page layout by PerfecType, Nashville, Tennessee

LeRoy, Matthew.
    Kingdom tide : unleashing the ripple effect of awakening / Matt LeRoy. – Frankin, Tennessee : Seedbed Publishing, ©2018.

    pages ; cm. – (Awakening series ; volume 3)

    ISBN 9781628245950 (paperback)
    ISBN 9781628246520 (Mobi)
    ISBN 9781628246537 (ePub)
    ISBN 9781628246544 (uPDF)

    1. Devotional calendars. 2. Meditations. 3. Spiritual exercises. 4. Religious awakening--Christianity. I. Title. II. Series. III. LeRoy, Matthew. IV. Walt, John David.

BV4810.L47 2018   260   2018955413

Seedbed

SEEDBED PUBLISHING
Franklin, Tennessee
seedbed.com

CONTENTS

why discipleship bands?

In his final hours, Jesus prayed specifically for us, "that all of them may be one, Father, just as you are in me and I am in you. May they also be in us so that the world may believe that you have sent me" (John 17:21).

Jesus prayed for the relationships between his followers to be of the very same character of the relationships between Father, Son, and Holy Spirit. Further, he prayed that our relationships would themselves find their home within the relationships of Father, Son, and Holy Spirit. Finally, note why this matters so much. Our relationships with each other will either lead people closer to God or further away.

Why discipleship bands? Because banded discipleship creates the context for the supernatural love of God to become real in our lives and through our relationships for the world. Discipleship bands all at once create space for inward transformation and outward mission.

The great tragedy of Christian discipleship is that it has come to mean so many things it can mean next to nothing. To be sure, there are complexities to discipleship, but at the core we must have deep clarity. In his final instructions to us, Jesus made it clear:

> *"All authority in heaven and on earth has been given to me. Therefore go and make disciples of all nations, baptizing them in the name of the Father and of the Son and of the Holy Spirit, and teaching them to obey everything I have commanded you. And surely I am with you always, to the very end of the age."* (MATT. 28:18-20)

We are to make disciples and teach them to obey everything Jesus has commanded us.

Let's be clear. We are not talking about a new small-group program, or better accountability groups, or Bible study groups. We do not fail at the mission of God in the world for lack of more information or better content or enhanced skills. We fail for a lack of love. Our foremost challenge is not learning more but loving more.

We like the way our friend Phil Meadows describes discipleship bands:

> *A band is a form of fellowship that is a means of charismatic encounter with the presence, leading, and power of the Holy Spirit. We come together. Jesus Christ is present as he has promised and he breathes his Spirit powerfully. And we come to help one another fix our eyes on him, in our midst. And we come to help one another open wide our mouths to receive the Spirit he gives. And we come to have holy conversation.*

The success of the gospel of Jesus Christ rises and falls on the strength of the relationships among his followers. Jesus' ambition is not to create a bunch of autonomous individual miracle workers. His mission is to create miraculous communities. This happens very simply through the arduous journey of people learning to love one another in the very same way that the Father and the Son and the Holy Spirit love one another.

There's nothing new here. It's actually quite ancient. From Jesus' band of disciples to the present day, everywhere the church has flourished some manner of banded discipleship was at the heart of it.

Most of us aren't lazy in our faith. We are stuck. It is not that we lack commitment. We are simply arrested in our development. The way forward is as close as a few other people who are willing to band together.

what is a
discipleship band?

A discipleship band is a group of three to five people who read together, pray together, and meet together to become the love of God for one another and the world.

Carefully consider this visionary text of Scripture from Paul's letter to the Ephesians.

> *I pray that out of his glorious riches he may strengthen you with power through his Spirit in your inner being, so that Christ may dwell in your hearts through faith. And I pray that you, being rooted and established in love, may have power, together with all the Lord's holy people, to grasp how wide and long and high and deep is the love of Christ, and to know this love that surpasses knowledge— that you may be filled to the measure of all the fullness of God.* (3:16-19)

First, note this is the Word of God. Second, it is a prayer. Third, it is all about relationships. For these reasons and more, it serves as a foundational text for our work. Discipleship bands provide a context where we can do these three things well. We read together. We pray together. We meet together. And we do these things with the all-consuming goal of being "filled to the measure of all the fullness of God." This is the way toward becoming the love of God for one another and the world.

WHY SO SMALL?

It's not that reading and praying and meeting can't happen in a larger group. The point of a discipleship band is the depth and quality of discipleship possible in a micro-community model. In truth, there are only so many people one can connect with on this level of intentionality. When it comes time to meet together, it is most effective to allot at least twenty minutes for each person (to share and be prayed for). In our experience, five member bands are not advisable; two-hour meetings become difficult to manage.

WHY SAME GENDER?

While sin is common to the human race, at times it takes on different character and qualities when it comes to different genders. Because of the way shame accompanies sin it can give rise to complicated dynamics between women and men. On the one hand, mixed gender groups can hinder vulnerability because of the presence of shame. On the other hand, vulnerable sharing can create inappropriate bonding. A discipleship band must be an ever-growing place of safety, where shame can be shed and truth can be told. Anything that tends to hinder this should be avoided. While mixed gender bands are permissible, in our judgment they are not advisable.

WHY SO SIMPLE?

Small groups satisfy many needs across the span of one's life. Discipleship bands provide a focused context for depth discipleship over a significant span of time. They aren't intended to be mission or service oriented. They aim to prepare people for mission by causing the mission of the gospel to become more deeply realized in one's own life.

Discipleship begins with understanding what God has done for us. It moves to God doing this work in us. Finally, it matures as God does this work through us in the world. Many programmatic models skip over the second phase, moving people from an understanding of what God has done for us to people doing something for God. The big challenge of discipleship centers around the work of God in us.

Because it's easier to measure and report outside activity, and because it is so difficult to measure the transformation of one's deepest self, and because there is so much desperate need all around us, it is tempting to skip the inside work and cut straight to the action part. Lest we establish a false dichotomy, let's be clear—discipleship is both inside and outside. The established tendency has been to skip the former to get to the latter, resulting in a brand of mission work that is helpful but shallow, well-intentioned but self-interested.

WHY SO DIFFICULT?

Most of us are arrested in our discipleship development. We get stuck repeating the same patterns of sin. We have believed lies about God and ourselves and they hold us like a prison with bars we can't see. Depth discipleship is hard because human beings have an unfortunate and almost infinite propensity to deceive themselves. The prophet Jeremiah said it best.

> *The human heart is the most deceitful of all things, and desperately wicked. Who really knows how bad it is?*
> (JER. 17:9 NLT)

Despite our best intentions, the reason we are stuck is we do not have the kinds of relationships it takes to catalyze and sustain the kind of work the Holy Spirit wills to do in our lives. This kind of soul work requires an ever-growing honesty with oneself; the kind of honesty that is next to impossible apart from a few other people alongside. It is why we must band together.

what do
discipleship bands do?

1. Bands Read Together

*The grass withers, the flower fades, but the word of our
God will stand forever.* (ISA. 40:8 ESV)

We are a people of One Book. The Word of God is both our
constitution and compass. Though a discipleship band is not a
Bible study group, one of the ways we band together is through
reading a common text. John Wesley once famously wrote this
stinging admonition in a letter to a certain Mr. John Premboth.

> *Whether you like it or not, read and pray daily. It is for
> your life; there is no other way; else you will be a trifler
> all your days, and a petty, superficial preacher. Do justice
> to your own soul; give it time and means to grow. Do not
> starve yourself any longer. Take up your cross and be a
> Christian altogether. Then will all children of God rejoice
> (not grieve) over you in particular.[1]*

---

1   Taken from an editorial by J. B. Chapman in *The Preacher's Magazine* (vol. 6, no. 1,
January 1, 1931). The note was written to John Premboth on August 17, 1760.

There are many ways to go about reading together. What matters is finding a way to get on the same page of Scripture together. Our common text does not function as the centerpiece of the band, rather it serves in a circumferential fashion to further band the group together.

2. Bands Pray Together

Devote yourselves to prayer, being watchful and thankful.
(COL. 4:2)

Our commitment is to watch over one another in love, to be for one another, and to encourage one another and build each other up. Our ongoing prayer life is a fundamental and foundational way we nurture these commitments. Band mates are prayer partners. We pray together in our weekly meeting, but even when we lift one another up throughout the week, we are, in effect, praying together. Over time band mates will know one another in extraordinary ways and will develop the capacity to pray for each other like few others in our lives can.

Every week in the band meeting, each person will have an opportunity to pray for another and to be prayed for. These times of prayer, perhaps more than anything else, will serve to strengthen the bonds of the band in deeply meaningful ways.

3. Bands Meet Together

Let us hold unswervingly to the hope we profess, for he who promised is faithful. And let us consider how we may spur one another on toward love and good deeds, not giving up meeting together, as some are in the habit of doing, but encouraging one another—and all the more as you see the Day approaching. (HEB. 10:23-25)

A discipleship band has not banded together until it is regularly meeting together. Meeting together is the most critical component of the discipleship band experience. Finding a time when everyone can consistently meet together can be challenging, but in our experience, a consistent time each week works best.

Aim for four meetings a month, but you can settle for a minimum of three. If it slips to two, the meeting time should be reconsidered. This highlights the problem with setting a meeting frequency of less than weekly. Meetings inevitably get cancelled, and when this happens within a bi-weekly or monthly approach it hurts the efficacy of the band.

Meeting together can take on a variety of formats. Face-to-face is obviously the best option, but a video-chat or phone call also works fine. Some bands find themselves all living in different places, making a face-to-face meeting impossible. They meet by conference call or video-chat and work toward an annual in-person retreat together. The point is to do what works and whatever it takes.

"Again, truly I tell you that if two of you on earth agree about anything they ask for, it will be done for them by my Father in heaven. For where two or three gather in my name, there am I with them." (MATT. 18:19-20)

how to use this book

You hold in your hands a resource designed specifically for a discipleship band. It facilitates the threefold work of a band to read together, pray together, and meet together. It is recommended for band members to read one of the entries each day, allowing it to guide your praying for one another and otherwise keep you reading a common text. Keep in mind, this is not meant to be a study curriculum proper. These readings are not meant to be the centerpiece of the weekly meeting but rather they are meant to keep a band on the same page throughout the week. Perhaps it will provide fodder for a group's informal interactions in any given week. Your band can elect to cover anywhere from five to seven readings per week at your own discretion.

On page 62 of this book you'll find a guide to conduct the discipleship band meeting, which you will find helpful as you meet together.

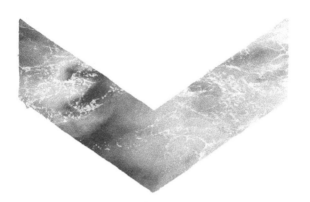

kingdom tide

WEEK ONE

orientation

1. DISSATISFIED

READ

Blessed are those who hunger and thirst for
*   righteousness,*
for they will be filled. (MATT. 5:6)

REFLECT

Blessed are the hungry and thirsty? Jesus is the man who calls himself the bread of life, feeds the multitudes, claims to be the source of internal streams of water, and commissions his followers to feed the sheep and extend a cup of cold water in his name. But here he says, "Blessed are those who hunger and thirst." Seems a touch off message for Jesus.

But Jesus doesn't want to simply still your appetite or numb your thirst. He wants to train and direct it toward him—the only thing that will truly satisfy. His vision for you is not a comfortably full belly, but a primal craving and hunger for what is needed most, what will fill to overflowing. His intention is not a refined palate, but a perpetual desire to draw from the deep well of holy love and divine righteousness.

3

Jesus, strange as it seems, wants you to be dissatisfied—with the things that are too small to fill out your soul or too low to reach true depth. Why? So that in the end, you learn that your oldest and persisting longings come to rest in him. Blessed are those who hunger and thirst for righteousness, for they will be filled.

PRAY

Jesus, make me hungry. Please don't let me settle for satisfaction in anything but you. Awaken my deepest longing and keep me dissatisfied until my appetite is trained on you.

CONFERENCE

Are you <u>satisfied</u> or dissatisfied? In what ways? What is it that you want most? *To grow deeper in Jesus –*

2. DEEPER

READ

"You are the light of the world. A town built on a hill cannot be hidden. Neither do people light a lamp and put it under a bowl. Instead they put it on its stand, and it gives light to everyone in the house. In the same way, let your light shine before others, that they may see your good deeds and glorify your Father in heaven." (MATT. 5:14-16)

REFLECT

When we think of going deeper, we are often actually dreaming of going higher. We equate spiritual depth with a spiritual high. So we seek a deeper relationship with Jesus and imagine it will result in an elevation of ourselves—lifting us up above the fray of struggle and difficulty.

Where did we get that idea? Partially, it comes from a consumer Christian model that promises this depth and height as a two-for-one deal—the closer you get to Jesus, the further you get from hardship. Or so the marketing department says. It also comes to us by virtue of our humanity. This is the oldest temptation, replayed again. There is another way, it whispers, and it includes a shortcut around surrender.

This manner of thinking has a subtle and seductive way of refocusing the spotlight. It edges us and our own needs and dreams and fears out onto center stage. Like the former celebrity willing to stoop to nearly any level of indignity for fifteen more minutes of attention, we impulsively look for ways to rise up, rather than lay down our lives. We want to make Jesus famous. But we secretly hope he will return the favor.

You are the light of the world, Jesus says. But don't get it twisted. The light is not on us. It is on him. We are a city set up on a hill. But he is the one who is elevated. The world is drawn to his light shining through us. But it is pointing them beyond us and illuminating the way to him.

PRAY

Jesus, you are the light of the world. And we commit to be your lanterns. Use us to lead others to you. We are not asking to be lifted up, but taken deeper. Elevate yourself for the world to see.

CONFERENCE

What are your thoughts on the distinction between spiritual depth and a spiritual high? How have you experienced each? How were they different?

3. DEPENDENCE

READ

"Enter through the narrow gate. For wide is the gate and broad is the road that leads to destruction, and many enter through it. But small is the gate and narrow the road that leads to life, and only a few find it." (MATT. 7:13-14)

REFLECT

Is the way of Jesus exclusive or inclusive?

Yep.

It is exclusive in its claim that the only way to God is through Jesus. It's inclusive in proclaiming that Jesus, God himself in the flesh, died on the cross for the redemption of the whole world. The gate is as narrow as God himself.

The gate is narrow. But the grace runs deep.

The road is narrow. But it stretches to the ends of the earth.

The gate into the kingdom is not what you have done for God, but what God has done for you. The road is not your record of right and wrong. The road is his righteousness. Our entrance into the kingdom is not dependent on how well we embody the teachings of Jesus. It is dependent on Jesus himself.

The gate to heaven left his throne. The road to God came to us.

It strikes me that the imagery is not only of a gate. It is also of a road. Both the gate and the road form one image together. It's a reminder that we don't simply stand inside the gate. This a journey that leads down that road, deeper into grace, deeper into dependence on Jesus. The same grace that found me, gripped me, saved me, forgave me, redeemed me, is still at work in me. The road leads us forward, step-by-step, move by move. Into the awakening.

PRAY

Jesus, you are the way—the one and only. You are the gate into the kingdom and the road into the Father's heart. Help me to remember my utter dependence on you in walking out my faith. You are the path beneath my feet, and every step forward depends on you.

CONFERENCE

In what ways have you depended on your own strength instead of on the grace of Jesus? What is one consistent part of your life that you struggle to relinquish to his control? What does it mean that Jesus uses imagery of both the gate and the road? How do they interplay?

4. DELIGHTED

READ

This, then, is how you should pray:
"Our Father in heaven,
hallowed be your name,
your kingdom come,
your will be done,
on earth as it is in heaven.
Give us today our daily bread.
And forgive us our debts,
as we also have forgiven our debtors.
And lead us not into temptation,
but deliver us from the evil one."
(MATT. 6:9-13)

REFLECT

Jesus says, "This, then, is how you should pray."

And with that, all of our deepest thoughts and eloquent musings on prayer come to a grinding halt. We silence our theory-crafting for a moment and lean in to listen.

The first two words of this seminal prayer set the framework for the rest of it. "Our Father." You sense his delight in these words, and in a profound move of tender mercy, Jesus pulls us into this divine intimacy of Father and child. Not only his Father, but our Father. He invites us to delight in that caring, protective, providing, nurturing love.

Admittedly, this language immediately creates distance for many of us. Instead of fostering intimacy, it raises a wall and carves a chasm between us and God. If he is a father, then many of us don't want anything to do with him. Will he abandon me too? Will he make promises he won't care to keep? Will he bring more scars, pain, lingering wounds?

For this reason, some advocate for dropping the imagery of God as Father. But I believe that's precisely why we so desperately need it. Perhaps the answer to a failed father is not the rejection of fatherhood, but the redemption of it. We carry that pain because instinctively we know what a good father should be like. And we mourn the death of that. Perhaps he is inviting us to discover the healing power of his Fatherhood in your life. A Father who never leaves, never breaks a promise, never hurts. A Father who cares and protects and cultivates. A Father who listens to our deepest hurts and dreams and shares in both. A Father who looks us in the eye and tells us that he loves us, believes in us, is proud of us.

Jesus invites us to delight in a father like that. He sees the pain that this word causes you. But instead of helping you avoid that pain, he offers to heal it.

PRAY

What other prayer could we pray today except the one Jesus taught us?

9

Our Father, in heaven, hallowed be your name, your kingdom come, your will be done, on earth as it is in heaven. Give us today our daily bread. And forgive our debts, as we also have forgiven our debtors. And lead us not into temptation, but deliver us from the evil one.

CONFERENCE

Have you experienced this childlike delight in the Father's love for you? If so, what fuels it? If not, what are the barriers? How does this image of God as Father land on your heart?

5. DEVOTED

READ

"You have heard that it was said, 'Love your neighbor and hate your enemy.' But I tell you, love your enemies and pray for those who persecute you." (MATT. 5:43-44)

REFLECT

This is the future of love. These words, these wild ideas that hum with revolution. This strange ordering of words that reorder the world as we know it. This is the future of love.

Jesus' provocative command to do the unthinkable—love your enemy—is often quoted and more often ignored. This is the unexplored frontier of the human experience.

Love your enemy is not hyperbole or poetry or a clever figure of speech. It is a defining commandment of this covenant community of Jesus.

But isn't this a hard teaching?

No. It's not hard. It's impossible.

Christianity is brilliant as a philosophy. It is a beautiful ethic of life. But as such it is utterly impossible. It is a yoke of bondage and brutal burden as mere religion. But thankfully, it is none of those things. It is a dynamic relationship with Jesus in which we are transformed, rescued, and reconciled by his holy love. But it doesn't stop there. His love for us creates our love for him, which in turn gives birth to that hallmark of the real Christian—devoted love for our neighbors, and yes, even our enemies. These words seem more ridiculous now than ever. Which is why we so desperately need them. And the future belongs to those who live them out.

But how?

After giving us this most impractical and revolutionary command to love our enemies, Jesus also carves out for us a most practical path. How can I love them? Start here: pray for them.

Prayer is more than talking. It's listening. Yes, in prayer we give our burdens to Jesus. But as we listen, he starts to give his burdens to us.

He will begin to show you how he sees that enemy of yours—and will begin to pull back the curtain on your own motives and attitudes.

Prayer for our enemies cultivates holy love for our enemies. Which actually destroys our enemies. Because once you begin to pray for them, and in turn love them, they can no longer be your enemies.

PRAY

Jesus, we pray for our enemies. We call by name the people who have hurt us, who have undercut us, who want to see us fail, who have lied about us. We pray for those who have betrayed us, who threaten us. We pray for those we want to hate. And we ask that your love would overpower, uproot, and replace the hate and hurt in our hearts.

CONFERENCE

What is your response to this teaching of Jesus? Do you think he is using a clever phrase or that he actually means it? What does that mean for us? Who is one person you will pray for?

WEEK TWO
DISSATISFIED

1. JOHN 4:13-15

READ

Jesus answered, "Everyone who drinks this water will be thirsty again, but whoever drinks the water I give them will never thirst. Indeed, the water I give them will become in them a spring of water welling up to eternal life."

The woman said to him, "Sir, give me this water so that I won't get thirsty and have to keep coming here to draw water."

REFLECT

The desert makes you thirsty. The heat dries up the soul, and the empty promises of satisfaction turn out to be nothing more than a mirage. There comes a turning point when discontent and dissatisfaction awaken desire and only the *real* thing will do.

The desert life of the woman at the well has been examined countless times, and she's been chastised for her promiscuous record of jumping from one bed to the next, scoring five husbands, and then shacking up with a man who was not even her husband.

But is that what was happening here? Look again. What rights did women have in this culture and time? None. They were seen as the property of the men in their lives, first their fathers and then their husbands. And the husband could cast out the wife for nearly any reason he wanted.

So perhaps what we have here is a woman who has been rejected and cast aside by the people in life she counted on the most. Promise after promise, broken and empty, a mirage in the desert. She was disappointed, dissatisfied, desperate. Thirsty for the real thing. In Jesus, she found every promise fulfilled and overflowing.

PRAY

Jesus, you are the living water and the only thing to satisfy my thirst. Keep me dissatisfied with anything but the real thing.

CONFERENCE

What thirst tends to lead you astray? What empty promise and mirage seems most enticing to you? Why?

2. ECCLESIASTES 2:10-11

READ

I denied myself nothing my eyes desired;
I refused my heart no pleasure.
My heart took delight in all my labor,

> and this was the reward for all my toil.
> Yet when I surveyed all that my hands had done
>   and what I had toiled to achieve,
> everything was meaningless, a chasing after the wind;
>   nothing was gained under the sun.

REFLECT

Waking up can feel like dying. So we continue to turn to distractions, coping mechanisms, and numbing habits in order to hold the awakening at bay. We set our eyes on alternative promises and pleasures, watch as they wave before us. We hypnotize ourselves: "You're getting very sleepy."

But the time has come to wake up. The quiet voice of the Holy Spirit cuts through the static and noise. That dissatisfaction that haunts you is more than a crisis. It's an invitation. Discontent can be a holy thing. It's the nagging realization that consumerism has failed you. There must be another way.

It's time to stop chasing the wind. It's time to stop saying yes to everything and give your yes to one thing. It's an all-encompassing, life-defining yes. It's a yes that unleashes a thousand smaller nos.

Jesus' call to self-denial isn't actually about the self at all. It's about him, and the confession that he is your everything. He is your yes, and everything else falls under his rule and reign.

PRAY

Holy Spirit, teach me to hear your quiet voice cutting through the distractions. Teach me to give one life-defining yes.

CONFERENCE

What distractions threaten to lull you asleep? In what area of your life are you holding back your yes?

3. MATTHEW 16:13-16

READ

When Jesus came to the region of Caesarea Philippi, he asked his disciples, "Who do people say the Son of Man is?"

They replied, "Some say John the Baptist; others say Elijah; and still others, Jeremiah or one of the prophets."

"But what about you?" he asked. "Who do you say I am?"

Simon Peter answered, "You are the Messiah, the Son of the living God."

REFLECT

This is a turning point in the gospel of Matthew. It changes the trajectory of the rest of the book. In two parts we see the beginnings of awakening, as once-closed eyes slowly start to flicker open. But sleepy eyes don't automatically adjust to the light.

First, we have the confession. Against the backdrop of Caesarea Philippi, Jesus asks his disciples, "Who do you say I am?" The setting is important because it is home to a massive rock face that housed a collection of shrines to competing gods and religious allegiance. Piercing through these crowded claims to the throne, Peter says, "You are the Messiah, the Son of the living God." For a moment, he sees clearly and articulates this foundational confession upon which the church will be constructed.

Second, we see the cross. Peter sees that Jesus is the Christ, but he can't yet see that means a cross. So his confession turns into a rebuke and protest because the cross is disorienting and reorders the way we see power. Peter was satisfied by his confession, but disgruntled by its meaning. He assumed the Messiah would be a military leader overthrowing the oppressive Roman Empire, not dying at its hands like an insurgent enemy of the state. He could not grasp the incongruity between his concept of power and this counter way of Jesus. The gap between empire and kingdom created a dissonance he could not harmonize.

How often have we experienced the same? Through revelation our eyes are opened to the truth. But we cannot yet grasp the implications. We are waking up. But our eyes have not yet adjusted to the light.

PRAY

Jesus, we confess that you are the Christ. And we know that means a cross. Help us to see clearly enough to trust you in the journey, even if it is disorienting for us.

CONFERENCE

Who is Jesus to you? In what ways are your eyes still adjusting to the light of that revelation?

4. LAMENTATIONS 3:22-26

READ

Because of the LORD's great love we are not consumed,
*   for his compassions never fail.*
They are new every morning,
*   great is your faithfulness.*
I say to myself, "The LORD is my portion,
*   therefore I will wait for him."*

The LORD is good to those whose hope is in him,
*   to the one who seeks him;*
it is good to wait quietly
*   for the salvation of the LORD.*

REFLECT

Lamentations is a funeral song, thick with grief and tragedy and wailing. It is heavy with mourning and weeping. It is an honest and raw reflection on the bitter afflictions that Jerusalem endured. Three waves of Babylonian destruction on the heels of Judah's rebellion. God will never break his covenant, but his broken people have a pattern of disobedience, forgetting their rescue and running headlong into defeat.

Lamentations is a collection of five distinct poems of lament, represented as five chapters in our English Bibles. Chapters 1, 2, 4, and 5 each contain twenty-two verses. Each verse of these chapters (except the concluding chapter 5) begins with a letter of the Hebrew alphabet in succession.

But what about chapter 3? Does it repeat the pattern? No. It triples the pattern. There are sixty-six poetic lines in chapter 3, located at the center of this collection. And what happens at the center of this central chapter? Here in the verses we catch the only glimpse of hope we find in the entire book. This book begins and ends with gut-wrenching lament. But even in the midst of that reality we find this one unshakable hope: great is God's faithfulness. Our hope is not in the promise that our situation will change. Our hope is in the promise that God will never change.

PRAY

Father, you are my unchanging hope. Your faithfulness is the one thing that holds firm as everything on either side of it gives way.

CONFERENCE

What is your lament? What tragedy or trial do you mourn? How has God been faithful in the midst of that?

5. 2 CORINTHIANS 4:16-18

READ

Therefore we do not lose heart. Though outwardly we are wasting away, yet inwardly we are being renewed day by day. For our light and momentary troubles are achieving for us an eternal glory that far outweighs them all. So we fix our eyes not on what is seen, but on what is unseen,

*since what is seen is temporary, but what is unseen is
eternal.*

REFLECT

Can you feel the shift in perspective and purpose captured in
these words? Can you sense the change?

For the past several days we have come face-to-face with the
reality of a nagging dissatisfaction with the way things are.
And we've unearthed and named the undercurrent of hunger
and thirst for the way they could be. A longing for more. Not
more in a consumeristic, generic sense, but more in the most
particular and singular way. To know and experience and
awaken to the one and only Way—the Father, Son, and Holy
Spirit.

And here in these words of Paul, we find vocabulary to artic-
ulate the change in our mode of seeing the world.

We take heart as the veil falls from the eyes of our hearts
and we begin to glimpse the counter story in which we find
ourselves. The discontent was not a barrier to hope, but a
guide into it. The cognitive dissonance was a realization of the
deeper way. The hunger and thirst were training our affections
and appetites and even allegiances around the unseen, eternal,
renewing glory so full of weight and authenticity that the very
burdens that threatened to crush and destroy now seem light
and momentary.

There has been a shift. A move of the soul to embrace dissatisfaction instead of fear it. And somehow it has lost its power
to confuse and has begun to clarify. It ceases to distract and

now harnesses focus. Even the slow shock of our own outward wasting away is a prophetic declaration of our inward renewal. The wasting will come to a mournful end. <u>But the renewing will go on from glory to glory. And so, friends, we do not lose heart</u>.

PRAY

Jesus, continue the shift that you have started in us. Help us to see the unseen work you are cultivating in us. Help us surrender to the inner renewal you have set in motion.

CONFERENCE

Do you resonate with a sense of dissatisfaction with the way things are? Why or why not? What new understanding stood out to you the most over this past week?

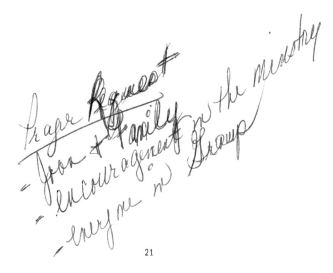

Gil's Employe's

WEEK THREE

DEEPER

---

1. PSALM 27:4

READ

One thing I ask from the LORD,
*   this only do I seek:*
that I may dwell in the house of the LORD
*   all the days of my life,*
to gaze on the beauty of the LORD
*   and to seek him in his temple.*

REFLECT

Let's get gut-level honest here. What do you seek? What is your one thing? What is your deepest desire? If you could be given one thing right now, and that one thing could be anything at all, what would you reach for? What is the one thing that could change your life forever? A financial wind-fall? A restored relationship? A shot at the spotlight? A chance to go back and try again?

One hallmark of the deeper life is a singular desire for one thing. Namely, the Lord himself. Not the collateral benefits of the relationship. Not the promise of blessing. But to dwell, rest, abide at home with him and in him, now and forever.

In a world that promises anything and everything, Jesus commands us to pursue one thing. The way toward anything and everything is guaranteed as the path of least resistance. But the way of one thing is the path of most significance.

We must learn to desire less and at the same time, more.

A sanctified and set-apart hunger fixed on the core thing. A baptized and transformed longing to gaze on the beauty of the Lord. Not to dart back and forth, eyes momentarily seizing on this glitter and that gold.

But to gaze.

On the beauty.

Of the Lord.

And find in him our deepest desire awakened and amplified and fulfilled.

PRAY

Father, Son and Holy Spirit, you are the one thing we seek. We long for you, and even though you fulfill all of our longings, we pray that you will never let us stop seeking more of you.

CONFERENCE

What do you seek? What is your one thing? What stands in the way? *Busness, for getting to slow and to dwell with God — time —*

2. PHILIPPIANS 3:7-11

READ

But whatever were gains to me I now consider loss for the sake of Christ. What is more, I consider everything a loss because of the surpassing worth of knowing Christ Jesus my Lord, for whose sake I have lost all things. I consider them garbage, that I may gain Christ and be found in him, not having a righteousness of my own that comes from the law, but that which is through faith in Christ—the righteousness that comes from God on the basis of faith. I want to know Christ—yes, to know the power of his resurrection and participation in his sufferings, becoming like him in his death, and so, somehow, attaining to the resurrection from the dead.

REFLECT

"I want to know Christ." We can all resonate with Paul on this one. There is a deep hunger to move into ever-expanding knowledge of and intimacy with Christ. We feel our souls begin to surge with an emphatic amen of agreement. And then he takes it even further: "and the power of his resurrection." Now I'm really with you, Paul. I want that. I long to move and operate and love and lead out of that kind of power. The dynamic reality of Jesus' resurrection at work in me, pushing back the signs of death all around me, the light of the empty tomb swallowing up the darkness? That's what I signed up for. I want to know more and more of that. You're on a roll, Paul. What's your next prayer?

". . . and participation in his sufferings, becoming like him in his death." Oh. Okay. Is there another option? Perhaps an alternative route that could navigate us around that unfortunate path? No. Never.

The way of Jesus leads to and through the cross. He promised us that up front. Before the cross carried any religious significance as a symbol or metaphor, when it only meant death, he plainly told us that to answer the call to follow him was to embrace his cross. If you want to know him and the power of his resurrection, then you must share in the fellowship of his sufferings and even his death. Once again, we learn that the counterintuitive way of the kingdom is descent. The direction of deeper is down.

PRAYER

Jesus, I do want to know you. In every way. Not only your resurrection, but your suffering and death as well. Teach me what it means to share in all of you.

CONFERENCE

What scares you most about following Jesus? What are you afraid this will cost?

3. PSALM 42:5-7

READ

Why, my soul, are you downcast?
Why so disturbed within me?
Put your hope in God,
for I will yet praise him,
my Savior and my God.

My soul is downcast within me;
therefore I will remember you
from the land of the Jordan,
the heights of Hermon—from Mount Mizar.
Deep calls to deep
in the roar of your waterfalls;
all your waves and breakers
have swept over me.

REFLECT

This famous psalm begins with a more famous image.

"As the deer pants for streams of water," the poet wrote, "so my soul pants for you, my God. My soul thirsts for God, for the living God" (vv. 1–2).

This is often depicted as a peaceful scene. But in truth, it is a scene of desperation. The downcast soul is parched for a sense of God's presence. Instead of quenching that thirst, the poet says that all he tastes are his own tears.

Pause right there. How does that description land on your heart? How does it speak to your own experiences?

The scene then takes a turn for the worse, moving from the language of desperation to outright danger. In the rocky hill country of Israel, the dry valley can quickly become a dangerous place during the rainy season. As rain runs down into the dry valley, it turns into a stream. Sounds refreshing. But the stream rapidly becomes a deadly channel of fast-flowing water, a barreling wall of waves that rush over and wash away anything in its path.

Let's pause again. Perhaps this imagery resonates as well. When you read, "Deep calls to deep in the roar of your water-falls; all your waves and breakers have swept over me," you don't envision a stroll on the beach. Instead, you see what the poet likely intended—the fear of being crushed and buried by the weight of it all.

You are not alone. How many of the poets and prophets, kings, and catalysts of the Scripture narrative wrestled with the same? How many of them experienced a deeper journey that drove them downward? But like them, don't deny the reality you're facing. Instead, remember the hope that will hold you through it.

PRAY

Our souls thirst for you, God. But at times we confess that we feel as if we will be crushed by the weight of it all. Help us to trust you with our most honest desperation, and allow the weight to drive us deeper into you.

CONFERENCE

What weight threatens to take you down? Do you perceive a way that it can drive you deeper into God?

4. 1 JOHN 3:1-3

READ

See what great love the Father has lavished on us, that we should be called children of God! And that is what we are! The reason the world does not know us is that it did not know him. Dear friends, now we are children of God, and what we will be has not yet been made known. But we know that when Christ appears, we shall be like him, for we shall see him as he is. All who have this hope in him purify themselves, just as he is pure.

REFLECT

The central hope of the gospel and, indeed, the full scope of Scripture is that we are rescued from the curse of sin, redeemed by the love of Jesus, renewed by the power of the Spirit, and even beyond that, reconciled to the heart of the Father. Not just for our own sake, but for the sake of his glory and expanding his family.

This is a radical idea. That God has always, since his first initiating act toward humanity, set out to form a family. And to draw us into it.

family of God

Through Adam and Eve, Noah and his offspring, Abraham and Sarah, Moses and Israel, David and the kings, all the way to a dusty nowhere town and a couple of nobodies named Joseph and Mary.

What a thought. If there is a God of any kind anywhere, anyone would imagine this deity setting out to create a kingdom of servants around its own exalted throne. That's pretty much the script of every religion everywhere. But the prevailing narrative has now been turned on its head. This God has called us sons and daughters, and our inheritance is his love. And as you can hear in John's own words, the world has yet to recover from the absurd surprise of it all.

If there is a God, you would assume that he is great.

The shocking twist is that he is good.

PRAY

Our Father, help us remember that this journey toward awakening is a journey deeper into the bonds of your family.

CONFERENCE

What does it mean to you to be a member in the family of God? How does that change the way you engage with your church, this group, and other relationships?

5. HEBREWS 10:19-23

READ

Therefore, brothers and sisters, since we have confidence to enter the Most Holy Place by the blood of Jesus, by a new and living way opened for us through the curtain, that is, his body, and since we have a great priest over the house of God, let us draw near to God with a sincere heart and with the full assurance that faith brings, having our hearts sprinkled to cleanse us from a guilty conscience and having our bodies washed with pure water. Let us hold unswervingly to the hope we profess, for he who promised is faithful.

REFLECT

"Confidence" and "Most Holy Place" are not words that should fit well together in the same sentence. In fact, the Most Holy Place was so revered, so respected, seen as so intensely and utterly holy that no one was ever allowed to enter it except on the holiest of occasions. Only one priest on only one day of the year was allowed to go in. And when he did, he wore bells on his robe and had a rope tied around his ankle. Why? Because the people were afraid the priest might drop dead under the weight of glory as he stepped into the presence of the Most Holy God. And if he did, no one would dare go in after him. If the bells fell silent, they would drag him out by the rope. Again, not exactly an image that inspires confidence.

Yet, we are told that because of the completed redemptive work of Christ, we may now enter into the Most Holy Place. Even more, because of Pentecost, the Holy Place has entered into us. We are moving, breathing temples, home to the holy God himself. This deeper life within us creates a sense of full assurance and confidence, and yet leads us into a total surrender and dependence.

PRAY

Holy God, make yourself at home in me and teach me to make myself at home in you. Fill me with confidence and assurance in your presence as your presence fills every part of me.

CONFERENCE

How does it change your view of your world to realize that the Holy God fills you? How does it change your home, work, relationships, community?

WEEK FOUR
DEPENDENCE

---

1. EPHESIANS 3:17-21

READ

. . . so that Christ may dwell in your hearts through faith. And I pray that you, being rooted and established in love, may have power, together with all the Lord's holy people, to grasp how wide and long and high and deep is the love of Christ, and to know this love that surpasses knowledge—that you may be filled to the measure of all the fullness of God.

Now to him who is able to do immeasurably more than all we ask or imagine, according to his power that is at work within us, to him be glory in the church and in Christ Jesus throughout all generations, for ever and ever! Amen.

REFLECT

How can you know something that is beyond knowledge? This seems like intentionally confusing mysticism or spiritual hyperbole. But Paul is not hiding something here. He's cracking open the door and inviting us to understand.

There's only one way to know something that is beyond knowledge. You experience it.

That's what he's getting at. He is inviting us to put down our roots and be established in this wide, long, high, deep love of Jesus. Through this rooting we will be infused with power that is beyond us. Our roots in this rich soil draw on the immeasurable as he fills us to the measure of the fullness of God. As the reach of the branches and the birth of the fruit are dependent on the roots and the soil, so our faith is utterly dependent on the one in whom we are rooted and established.

We should dream and innovate and pioneer. We should create and experiment and feel out the edges of what's next. But we must do this and all things out of being rooted and established. This will be the difference between branches stretching wide and high and becoming a tumbleweed blown by every breeze.

PRAY

Jesus, root me in the depth and width and height and length of love. Establish me in the experience of you that goes beyond what can be otherwise known. Let me know you and be filled with the fullness of the immeasurably more.

CONFERENCE

Have you ever experienced God in a way that goes beyond other forms of knowledge? Share with your group.

2. 1 SAMUEL 17:47

READ

"All those gathered here will know that it is not by sword or spear that the LORD saves; for the battle is the LORD's, and he will give all of you into our hands."

REFLECT

This famous declaration echoes from the Valley of Elah, where a young, anointed shepherd-king stood against a giant with no armor, no military weapon, only a sling and five smooth stones. It is an image that permeates our culture to this day. The quintessential tale of the underdog beating impossible odds. And time and again we return to this stream running through the valley, kneel next to David, and select enough courage to go and face our own giants. We draw strength from the common admonition to be as brave as David, and conquer every fear through faith.

But that is not what this story is about. It is not about us. We are not David in this narrative, mustering enough inspiration and heroism to topple the outsized circumstances that threaten to take us out. No, our place in the story is hiding behind Saul's or David's brother, too afraid to even step onto the battlefield.

Instead, David foreshadows another anointed Shepherd-King who will also use a peculiar and unconventional weapon to overcome the giants of sin and death. The battle belongs to him. It will not be won by sword (our strength) or spear (our strategy) but by his Spirit.

This prayer is not one of defiant boldness, but of confessed dependence. You, Lord, and you alone can win the battles we face. And, indeed, they have been won in advance. We do not dream of ascending to become the hero. We surrender to being but one small stone in your sling.

PRAY

Anointed Shepherd-King, every battle we face belongs to you. We trust you to overcome the giants we cannot. We declare that the battle belongs to you.

CONFERENCE

What battles are you facing right now? What keeps you from surrendering them the Lord?

3. HEBREWS 12:1-3

READ

Therefore, since we are surrounded by such a great cloud of witnesses, let us throw off everything that hinders and the sin that so easily entangles. And let us run with perseverance the race marked out for us, fixing our eyes on Jesus, the pioneer and perfecter of faith. For the joy set before him he endured the cross, scorning its shame, and sat down at the right hand of the throne of God. Consider

him who endured such opposition from sinners, so that
you will not grow weary and lose heart.

REFLECT

William Faulkner once wrote, "The salvation of the world is in man's suffering." Well, he was almost right. It is found in *one* man's suffering.

The cross of Jesus is the pivot point of salvation. And as it comes into view, he does not shrink back or change his course. He sets his face toward the cross and walks with resolve to his death and your life.

This passage is an invitation to embrace the suffering of Jesus and walk the long road with him to the cross. It is a reminder of our frailty and lack of power to save ourselves. We are dust and ash without him. And the writer challenges us to reflect on the reality of our sin, the cost of our salvation, and our utter dependence on the grace of Jesus.

This dependence is binding, and yet at the same time, it is miraculous freedom. The writer describes in magnificent language the liberty that comes to us through the triumphant suffering of Christ. As the pioneer drags his cross down the way of sorrows, he carves a path of victory in which we now run, with chains and shame broken and scattered in our wake. As the saints surround us, we fix our eyes on him and persevere in his joy. Each step he stumbled toward death quickens our pace and invigorates our journey. His suffering is our salvation, and our surrender is our victory in the race laid out for us.

PRAY

Pioneer and perfecter of our faith, carve the way for us. Give us strength to surrender, for even that ability comes from you. Keep my eyes fixed on you and my feet empowered run in your steps.

CONFERENCE

What is the sin that so easily entangles you? How is Jesus' victory on the cross overcoming that in your life? What distracts you from keeping your eyes fixed on Jesus?

4. DANIEL 6:10-12

READ

Now when Daniel learned that the decree had been published, he went home to his upstairs room where the windows opened toward Jerusalem. Three times a day he got down on his knees and prayed, just as he had done before. Then these men went as a group and found Daniel praying and asking God for help. So they went to the king and spoke to him about his royal decree: "Did you not publish a decree that during the next thirty days anyone who prays to any god or human being except to you, Your Majesty, would be thrown into the lions' den?"

REFLECT

It's important to realize that Daniel did not pray because it was his last resort. He prayed because it was his first priority. He didn't pray because there was nothing else he could do, but because it was what "he had always done before."

By the time of this story, Daniel was likely in his eighties. And long ago, as a teenager in Daniel 1, he resolved that his appetite, affection, and allegiance would be squarely rooted in one place. He created a pattern of dependence and trust in God that anchored him through the turmoil and disruptions of military defeat, forceful captivity, and a life of exile in a foreign empire.

We celebrate his moment of courage, but we should look to his pattern of dependence. Courage is not an outer quality. It is the inner life breaking out into the open. It is not honed in public, on a stage, in the big moment. It is slowly cultivated in the garden of the soul and is pushed and drawn to the surface by the Holy Spirit in the moment we need it.

Don't forget that Daniel was now second in command in the empire. He had great influence and proximity to power. Yet he did not look to the empire for his deliverance. He went to his room, opened his windows toward Jerusalem, and fixed his eyes on a kingdom he could not see. He had the vision to discern the alternative story and align his life with that script.

PRAY

Holy Spirit, teach us to resolve that our appetites, affections, and allegiance will always be rooted in you. Cultivate in us a pattern of dependence until it becomes our standard mode of operation and first response to every trial.

CONFERENCE

What is your first response in times of difficulty, stress, and trial? To whom or what do you look first? What does that say about your dependency?

5. JOSHUA 1:7

READ

"Be strong and very courageous. Be careful to obey all the law my servant Moses gave you; do not turn from it to the right or to the left, that you may be successful wherever you go."

REFLECT

Have you ever felt inadequate? In over your head? Not up to the task in front of you and afraid of failure? These thoughts surely passed through Joshua's mind as he inherited the mantle and ministry of Moses after his death. Poised to enter the land of promise and step into the realization of God's covenant with Israel, Joshua found the mission suddenly thrust on him following this tragic loss for God's people. Not only did he mourn the loss of a leader and friend; he had to shepherd the people beyond the point where Moses had led them.

In his own inadequacy, he met God's provision and discovered that the only way forward was utter dependence. "Be strong and courageous" was not a pep talk or pop theology designed to make him believe in himself. "Be strong and courageous" was a prophetic vision of what happens when God's people sink into a soul-level dependence on his strength instead of our own. The strength and courage spoken of here do not originate in us. They are borrowed. They well up within us but they come from outside of us. They are signs of awakening cultivated through that journey that starts with dissatisfaction and leads us deeper.

Joshua stood at a crossroads moment. It was the end of one journey and the beginning of the next. But to move forward he had to recognize his desperate need for dependence. Only then was he able to step forward in strength and courage.

PRAY

Jesus, remind me that my desperation for you can become dependence. Be my strength and courage when my weakness and fears hold me back.

CONFERENCE

Where are you feeling inadequate? Where do you feel underprepared or in over your head? Allow your group members to speak words of strength and courage.

WEEK FIVE

DELIGHTED

1. GENESIS 1:31

READ

God saw all that he had made, and it was very good. And there was evening, and there was morning—the sixth day.

REFLECT

God shows us how to delight. In this creation narrative of Genesis 1, all things spring from his genius overflowing from his love. And this concept of delight is one of those countless gifts he plants within us from our first moment of formation.

After his frenzy of creative grace poured out through forming the earth, carving the mountains, raising the forests, spilling the seas; after the stars above and the animals below; after the crown of creation, humanity made in his image; after all of this, his assessment is clear. He delights.

And he teaches us to do the same. This is our design and calling. It is woven into the fabric of the creative order, as natural as a bird's flight, or a star's light, or an orchard's fruit, or a baby's cry. We were made to delight in God.

In the Westminster Catechism, a teaching instrument conceived to disciple young and new believers in the way of Jesus, the very first question gets straight to this point. It asks, What is the chief end of humanity? What is our goal and purpose and design? The answer comes back: To glorify God and enjoy him forever.

This answer should not surprise us. God delighted in his creation. He was teaching us to delight in him in return. "It was very good," he said. "Only because you are," we answer. We were made to delight. And he went first to teach us the way.

PRAY

God, your creation was good only because you are. And every good thing comes from you. Teach us the way of delighting in all of the endless good in you.

CONFERENCE

What is good about God? What is it about him that is worthy of delight? Share with your group. Even better, share with him.

2. DEUTERONOMY 6:4–9

READ

Hear, O Israel: The LORD our God, the LORD is one. Love the LORD your God with all your heart and with all your soul and with all your strength. These commandments that I give you today are to be on your hearts. Impress them on your children. Talk about them when you sit at

*home and when you walk along the road, when you lie
down and when you get up. Tie them as symbols on your
hands and bind them on your foreheads. Write them on
the door frames of your houses and on your gates.*

REFLECT

This passage includes a prayer known as the *shema*. It takes
its name from the Hebrew term for "hear," the first word of the
prayer. The ancient Jewish community cherished this prayer
and made it an essential part of their daily rhythm of life,
repeating it every morning and evening. It became a way of
framing their day—indeed, their entire lives.

Tangled up in the dynamic meaning of the word is not only a
command but an assumed response to it. Hearing is only half
of the relationship. Its counterpart is a response of obedience.

To hear and obey is the complete command. And to whom
would Israel listen and respond? The Lord our God, who is
described as being one. This means he is unique, the one and
only true God. But he is also unified. He reigns over every
broken and fractured aspect of our lives. This is disruptive in a
time and place where the surrounding cultures have invented
a different deity for every compartment of life. With this
God, there are no tribal borders between the heart, mind, or
strength. He is one Lord and Lord of all.

The truest way of delighting in the Lord is to obey him in
our coming and going, at home and on the road, in our lying
down and rising up, by impressing it on our hearts and heads
and hands and expressing it through every word and deed. The

only way to love the Lord our God is with our whole hearts, minds, and strength. Holiness is full surrender to the unrivaled reign of Jesus over every part of who we are. It is all of you delighting in all of him.

PRAY

God who hears, teach us to attune our hearts to you. To not only hear but to respond in obedience. Lord who is one, help us to live a unified life, under the jurisdiction of your unrivaled reign.

CONFERENCE

What areas of your life are marked by a response of obedience? What areas are not?

3. ISAIAH 6:1-8

READ

In the year that King Uzziah died, I saw the Lord, high and exalted, seated on a throne; and the train of his robe filled the temple. Above him were seraphim, each with six wings: With two wings they covered their faces, with two they covered their feet, and with two they were flying. And they were calling to one another:

> *"Holy, holy, holy is the LORD Almighty;*
> *the whole earth is full of his glory."*

At the sound of their voices the doorposts and thresholds shook and the temple was filled with smoke.

"Woe to me!" I cried. "I am ruined! For I am a man of unclean lips, and I live among a people of unclean lips, and my eyes have seen the King, the LORD Almighty."

Then one of the seraphim flew to me with a live coal in his hand, which he had taken with tongs from the altar. With it he touched my mouth and said, "See, this has touched your lips; your guilt is taken away and your sin atoned for."

Then I heard the voice of the Lord saying, "Whom shall I send? And who will go for us?"

And I said, "Here am I. Send me!"

REFLECT

Vision is how we see the world. That's not exactly a ground-breaking thought. But we often go about our day-to-day business giving no consideration at all to the lens through which we perceive. What is our vision of the world? What is our vision for the present and future? More than what we see, we should ask, how do we perceive?

Isaiah received a vision. And it transformed his ability to see. It radically reordered the ways he viewed the past, present, and future. For a brief, life-quaking moment, the curtain was pulled back and he was able to catch a glimpse of the baseline reality of this universe—Yahweh is enthroned as the one and only God, unrivaled in his reign.

It revealed two things that seem contradictory at first. It infused Isaiah with desperation and delight. Desperation over his own sin and the sin of his people in light of this all holy

God. But it also generated delight because this all-holy God was cleansing them of that sin and clearly has the undisputed power to see them through anything they face as a people.

Isaiah is the prophet of desperation and delight. He warned of the coming captivity. And looked beyond to the arrival of deliverance. He proclaimed judgment for Israel's rebellion and sin. And declared that the Messiah is coming, with rescue and redemption in his wake.

This vision gave him a way to perceive. And he was never able to see the world in the same way again.

PRAY

Holy, holy, holy God, lifted high above all things, give us a vision of your glory by which we may see everything else.

CONFERENCE

What is your dominant vision of the world? How would you describe the view from where you stand?

4. MATTHEW 11:28-30

READ

"Come to me, all you who are weary and burdened, and I will give you rest. Take my yoke upon you and learn from me, for I am gentle and humble in heart, and you will find rest for your souls. For my yoke is easy and my burden is light."

REFLECT

My mom grew up on a little fishing village called Harkers Island, on the coast of North Carolina. From the front porch her dad built, you can see the Cape Lookout Lighthouse and a stretch of land in the sound called Shackleford Banks. Shackleford Banks is home to a population of wild horses. They have never been bridled, trained, or domesticated. Local authorities protect them from human interaction, preserving their untouched way of life. Historians and scientists believe their Spanish Mustang ancestors survived a shipwreck and swam to this strip of safety, where their family line has continued for hundreds of years.

When I was growing up, the wild horses on Harkers Island were a symbol of freedom in mind. No bridles. No saddles. No domestication for the purpose of human service. Total freedom. Until one day it dawned on me. Shackleford Banks is only a couple of miles wide and fewer than ten miles long. For hundreds of years this family line of wild horses has been restricted to this small stretch of sand and seagrass, surrounded by a boundary of water. Perhaps that is not freedom, but isolation.

When Jesus offers the yoke, the enemy whispers of freedom from it. What he really wants for you is isolation. A perceived freedom from Christ, which, of course, is merely bondage to yourself and your own enslaving sin. Jesus channels the prophet's hope of a God that shatters the yoke of slavery, and in its place he offers a yoke of freedom. Bound to him in discipleship, tied to him in intimacy, walking with him in rest and true fulfillment.

The island appears to be a promise of freedom. It is actually a legacy of isolation.

The yoke seems to be a form of bondage. It is actually an invitation to delight in the freedom of Jesus.

PRAY

Lord of the yoke, break us free from the bonds of slavery and the false promise that leads to isolation. Bind us to you. Draw us near, and teach us to rest in your freedom.

CONFERENCE

How does this imagery of the yoke strike you? Does it rub you wrong way? What do you think about this distinction between freedom and isolation.

5. LUKE 1:46-55

READ

And Mary said:

"My soul glorifies the Lord
    and my spirit rejoices in God my Savior,
for he has been mindful
    of the humble state of his servant.
From now on all generations will call me blessed,
    for the Mighty One has done great things for me—

holy is his name.
His mercy extends to those who fear him,
    from generation to generation.
He has performed mighty deeds with his arm;
    he has scattered those who are proud in their inmost
    thoughts.
He has brought down rulers from their thrones
    but has lifted up the humble.
He has filled the hungry with good things
    but has sent the rich away empty.
He has helped his servant Israel,
    remembering to be merciful
to Abraham and his descendants forever,
    just as he promised our ancestors."

REFLECT

Mary was the first of her kind, a pioneer of a new form of humanity—the Jesus bearers. Of course, the virgin birth is unique, utterly unprecedented and wholly unrepeated. But even in this singular miracle of human history, we see how it will change everything after. Because Mary bore the incarnate Jesus in her womb, we now bear him in our souls. The living God now lives in us.

Our tradition protested against the abuses of the papal institution and sought to reform the church in the image of its radical beginnings. So we tend to shy away from focusing on Mary out of fear of past misconceptions. But through this humble woman from a backwoods village, far out of the sphere of power, the Almighty draws near to us. As the baby kicks in her womb, empires tremble and giants lose their step. She delights in this strange mercy of God that exalts the humble and unseats rulers.

We bear this same revolutionary Jesus in us. And once again his presence in us threatens to upend the conventional order of things and usher in the way of the kingdom. In our cities and churches, he is sowing the seeds of a new revival that continue to arrive through unlikely vessels.

And like Mary, we delight in his strange wisdom. Our souls glorify his ever-extending faithfulness. Our spirits rejoice in his grace to us and through us. And we echo, "May it be to your servants as you have said."

PRAY

Jesus in us, use us to lift up the lowly, even if it means we are the ones who are humbled. Teach us to delight in this disruption of the organization chart and to rejoice in your strange mercy to the weak.

CONFERENCE

How is Jesus upending the status quo in your community? Does that image cause you to delight or despair? Why?

WEEK SIX
DEVOTED

---

1. ROMANS 13:8-10

READ

Let no debt remain outstanding, except the continuing debt to love one another, for whoever loves others has fulfilled the law. The commandments, "You shall not commit adultery," "You shall not murder," "You shall not steal," "You shall not covet," and whatever other command there may be, are summed up in this one command: "Love your neighbor as yourself." Love does no harm to a neighbor. Therefore love is the fulfillment of the law.

REFLECT

It requires a sharp mind to grasp what is complex. But genius exists in the ability to make the complex simple. This is never more evident than in the life and teaching of Jesus. When faced with the trap of naming the greatest commandment of the law, he brilliantly threaded the entire law together with the two-sided, yet single coin of holy love for God and neighbor. In insisting on naming two commands, not one, he shows us that love is like breathing. Which is more important, breathing in or breathing out? Pick one. You can't. If you're not doing both, soon enough you won't be doing either.

Paul follows his rabbi in this simple (though never simplistic) understanding of theology, declaring that holy love is the irreducible thread holding the fullness of the law and prophets together. And this genius is channeled yet again by John Wesley as he gives a plain account of the royal way of holiness. We'll give that radical Mr. Wesley the last word today:

> It were well you should be thoroughly sensible of this: the heaven of heavens is love. There is nothing higher in religion: there is, in effect, nothing else. If you look for anything but more love, you are looking wide of the mark, you are getting out of the royal way, and when you are asking others, "Have you received this or that blessing?" if you mean anything but more love, you mean wrong; you are leading them out of the way, and putting them upon a false scent.[2]

PRAY

God of love, form us in that likeness. Train us to breath in this rhythm of loving you and our neighbor.

---

2 John Wesley, *A Plain Account of Christian Perfection* (New York: New-York Methodist Tract Society, printed by James and John Harper, 1821), chap. 10, question 33, p. 36.

CONFERENCE

What do you think of this elevated vision of love? How does it resonate or conflict with your own view of God's character? How does it resonate or conflict with your own pattern of life?

2. MATTHEW 20:25-28

READ

Jesus called them together and said, "You know that the rulers of the Gentiles lord it over them, and their high officials exercise authority over them. Not so with you. Instead, whoever wants to become great among you must be your servant, and whoever wants to be first must be your slave—just as the Son of Man did not come to be served, but to serve, and to give his life as a ransom for many."

REFLECT

To put this passage in its context, the mother of James and John had just asked Jesus to elevate her sons to his right and left when he comes into his kingdom.

They got that he is a King with a kingdom. But they still couldn't grasp what kind of King and kingdom. And neither do we. There will, indeed, be people on his right and left when he is lifted up. But they will be two thieves crucified next to him. The cup Jesus will drink is not a crown or a throne. It is a cross and a yoke.

It's interesting that James and John were already in Jesus' inner circle. It seems this request was designed to undercut Peter and push him out of his place of influence and perceived highest rank. They wanted more than intimacy with Jesus; they wanted influence. More than proximity to him, they wanted power over the other disciples.

Jesus used this power grab to envision a counterintuitive path to greatness. It denies the pyramid organizational chart of hierarchy. Jesus says that in his kingdom, greatness is found by serving others. It is not defined by position, but by posture. And his own life carves out the way. Ask yourself, what official position did Jesus hold? What posture did he take?

Dr. Cornel West famously said, "Justice is what love looks like in public."[3] Likewise, I believe that service is what love looks like in private. Now go, be great, for the glory of God and the sake of others.

PRAY

Jesus, Servant King, teach us to live in a posture of service. Form in us true kingdom greatness for the glory of you and the sake of others.

CONFERENCE

Two questions:

1. Whom will you serve? (No vague categories. Name a specific person.)

2. How? (Get specific. Spell out actions you will take.)

---

3 Cornel West, "Justice Is What Love Looks Like in Public" (sermon, Howard University, Washington, DC, April 17, 2011).

3. 1 PETER 4:8-11

READ

Above all, love each other deeply, because love covers over a multitude of sins. Offer hospitality to one another without grumbling. Each of you should use whatever gift you have received to serve others, as faithful stewards of God's grace in its various forms. If anyone speaks, they should do so as one who speaks the very words of God. If anyone serves, they should do so with the strength God provides, so that in all things God may be praised through Jesus Christ. To him be the glory and the power for ever and ever. Amen.

REFLECT

Ask the average person, loosely familiar with the story and Jesus' life, and he or she will likely remember Peter most for one thing above all else. He denied Jesus. Yes, he was among the inner circle of disciples. He was the disciple who first articulated that foundational confession that Jesus is more than a prophet or teacher, but he is, in fact, the Christ, the very Son of the living God. Peter was the one who stepped out of the boat and onto the waves, who preached the inaugural sermon of the church at its birth, and who became a pioneer in the rising kingdom tide.

And yet we remember his denial above the rest. Why? Because in our way of keeping score, sin covers a multitude of love. But not so with Jesus.

After his resurrection, Jesus directly confronted this defining sin of Peter's life. With what? With love. "Peter, do you love me?" he asked. Not once, but three times. Jesus covered the one moment Peter would have died to have back with the moment he would never forget. "I love you," Peter affirmed, once for every time he had denied. And then, in the strength of this love and the power of the Holy Spirit, three thousand people joined the movement of Jesus as Peter preached at Pentecost. Three thousand. One thousand transformed lives for each of his denials.

"Love covers a multitude of sins," Peter wrote. This isn't poetry. It's experience. And once you've experienced it, you can't go on seeing others according to their defining sin. You will see them covered in thick layers of holy love, as Jesus beacons you to join him in piling it on.

PRAY

Jesus, thank you for your love. It has not only covered our sins but transformed our hearts. Please keep moving us into deeper awakening until we are defined by our devoted love for God and others.

CONFERENCE

Why do we remember Peter most for his defining failure? Name one defining trait for which you want to be remembered. Who do you see according to their defining sin? Name a different defining trait by which you can identify them instead.

4. 1 JOHN 4:18-19

READ

There is no fear in love. But perfect love drives out fear,
because fear has to do with punishment. The one who
fears is not made perfect in love. We love because he first
loved us.

REFLECT

As we move in this journey, from the desert of dissatisfaction to the awakening of devotion, every single step along the way has been initiated and navigated by the same love. It is the love of Jesus that provokes those pangs of discontent. One taste of its authenticity and we can never again settle for anything except the real thing. It is this love that invites and draws us deeper, descending to the cross and raising us up in resurrection. It is this love that roots and establishes us in utter dependence upon the Root of all things. It is this love that teaches us what it means to delight in the one who is love himself. And it is this love that works its way through us, leaving no part of us untouched and unchanged, welling up and over and out into the world around us in the form of profound love for others.

In a day and time when relationships are strained by fear and suspicion, holy love drives us out into the widening gaps. The people of Jesus are born from, filled with, and driven by holy love, and used to drive out fear in the communities around us. Because he did it first.

PRAY

Holy God of holy love, drive out fear and hate darkness. Light us on fire and let us burn to light the way.

CONFERENCE

Where is the fear in your community? Where does it come from? How can the holy love of Jesus drive it out and replace it?

5. PROVERBS 27:17

READ

As iron sharpens iron,
so one person sharpens another.

REFLECT

These are cherished words. We build men's ministry around them. We superimpose them over a nice photo and post it to social media as a shout-out to our friends. We print them on T-shirts and hang them on our walls or sell them on every cheesy knickknack imaginable down at the local Christian bookstore. We have memorized these words. But I think we have missed the image.

The imagery here is not designed to be sentimental or pretty. Instead the vision cast in these words is one of friction, heat, and the hard work of authentic community.

How does iron sharpen iron? Not by speaking limp platitudes of faux encouragement. Not by surface-level pleasantries. Iron sharpens iron through the painful process of friction, one piece in immediate contact with the other, leaning into each other for the purpose of improving both. It hurts. But it's one of the only ways to help.

Most of us claim to want authentic community. But we aren't willing to pay the price for it. We bail at the first sign of friction, assuming that's a red flag that the friendship isn't working. But friction is the only way a friendship can work. To be devoted in Jesus-like love for your friends means that you are willing to lean into each other. You are willing to endure the friction and speak the truth in love and fight for another for the long haul. And along the way, this Jesus-like love ends up sharpening us both.

PRAY

God of love, you designed us for relationship with you and each other. Teach us patience to lean into the friction of our friendships, and sharpen each other in the journey of discipleship.

CONFERENCE

How have the members of this group sharpened you in this journey? Share with one another, and express your gratitude.

the discipleship band meeting structure

The weekly band meeting is simple in structure and format. Budget for twenty minutes per person. Some small talk is fine, but the band must respect the time allotment. The meeting should be formally opened with the words below. Once this happens, it's band business to the end.

I. OPENING

One Voice: **Awake O Sleeper and Rise from the Dead.**
All Others: **And Christ Will Shine on You.**

(adapted from Ephesians 4:14)

PRAYER READ IN UNISON OR BY ONE MEMBER OF THE BAND

Heavenly Father, we pray that out of your glorious riches you would strengthen us with power through your Spirit in our inner being, so that Christ may dwell in our hearts through faith. And we pray that we, being rooted and established in love, may have power, together with all the Lord's holy people, to grasp how wide and long and high and deep is the love of Christ, and to know this love that surpasses knowledge—that we may be filled to the measure of all the fullness of God. We ask this in Jesus' name, amen.

(adapted from Ephesians 3:16–19)

II. THE QUESTIONS

1. How is it with your soul?
2. What are your struggles?
3. Any sin to confess?
4. Anything you want to keep secret?
5. How might the Holy Spirit be speaking and moving in your life?

In the interest of keeping it simple and memorable, think of the questions as: Soul, Struggles, Sin, Secrets, Spirit.

At the conclusion of each person's time of sharing, someone from the band will offer a prayer for the one who shared. This is also an opportunity to seek clarification, offer encouragement, and to speak into one another's lives.

It may be advisable for a new band, particularly among people unfamiliar with one another, for the first month to cover question #1 only. Perhaps add question #2 for the second month. Go at your own pace and pay attention to relational dynamics. Focus on building trust and always maintain confidentiality.

III. CLOSING

READ IN UNISON OR BY ONE MEMBER OF THE BAND

Now to him who is able to do immeasurably more than all we ask or imagine, according to his power that is at work within us, to him be glory in the church and in Christ Jesus throughout all generations, for ever and ever! Amen.

(Ephesians 3:20–21)